The Beasts That Vanish

Poems

Al Maginnes

⧟

Blue Horse Press   Redondo Beach, California   2021

THE BEASTS THAT VANISH

Poems

Al Maginnes

Blue Horse Press
Redondo Beach,
California

Copyright © 2021 by Al Maginnes
All rights reserved
Printed in the United States of America

Cover photo: "Diplomystus"©
Jeffrey C. Alfier

Editors: Jeffrey and Tobi Alfier
Blue Horse Press logo: Amy Lynn Alfier (1996)

ISBN   978-0-578-86292-7

The moral rights of the author have been asserted. No part of this book may be reproduced or transmitted in any form or by any means, electronic or mechanical, including photocopy, recording, or any information storage and retrieval system now known or to be invented, without permission in writing from the publisher, except by a reviewer who wishes to quote brief passages in connection with a review written for inclusion in a magazine, newspaper or broadcast.

FIRST EDITION © 2021

This and other Blue Horse Press titles may be found at www.bluehorsepress.com

※

For Jamie and Isabel

Acknowledgements

Bear Review: "Night Deer"; "Dream's Animals"
Blue Mountains Review: "The Night of Changing Fires," "Little Universe"
Boxcar Poetry Review: "Animals Invented By Longing"
Chariton Review: "The Jesus Year"
Cumberland River Poetry Review: "What the River Built"
decomP: "One Trouble With Stories"
Lake Effect: "Einstein's Violin" "The Wings Below Our Hearts"
Laurel Review: "As Much Salvation As One Can Believe"
Louisiana Literature: "How It Comes to Us"
The Meadow: "Shine," "Storms That Make Their Own Names"
Natural Bridge: "Leaves"; "Playlist for a Record Burning"
North American Review: "The Conversions of the Body"
North American Review Online: "Pumpkin Spice and the Infinite Horizon Blues"
Plume: "Shooting Pool in the Mental Hospital"
Rattle: "Stern"
San Pedro River Review: "Reading By the Moon" "The Beasts That Vanish"
Serving House Journal: "Ellipsis"
Shenandoah: "Renewal"
Slipstream: "Ghost Stories With Knives"
South Florida Poetry Journal: "Dice, Scripture and Lost Winnings: An Unfinished Portrait"
Spry: "Lottery Tickets and the Odds of Retirement: A Meditation"
Tar River Poetry: "Creed"
Terrain.org: "Landscape Rising Out of Solitude"
Vox Populi: "The Book of Forgetting"; "The Skeleton Parade"; "Source"
Wayfarer: "Exchange"
Xavier Review: "Counting Stock"

Contents

Part One

The Skeleton Parade	3
Shine	4
What the River Built	5
The Conversions of the Body	7
Reading By the Moon	9
The Book of Forgetting	11
Ghost Stories With Knives	13
What We Are Coming To	15
The Jesus Year	17
Landscape Rising From Solitude	19

Part Two

Animals Invented By Longing	25
The Beasts That Vanish	26
Night Deer	31
Judas Lightning	32
The Bird Born Out of Weather	34
Dream's Animals	36
Storms That Make Their Own Names	37

Part Three

Leaves	43
Exchange	45
Playlist for a Photograph of a Record Burning	47
Ellipsis	50
Source	53

Part Four

When We Burned the Diaries	57
Shooting Pool in the Mental Hospital	58
Dice, Scripture, and Lost Winnings:	
An Unfinished Portrait	62

Pumpkin Spice and the Infinite Horizon Blues	64
Counting Stock	67
Lottery Tickets and the Odds of Retirement: A Meditation	70

Part Five

The Night of Changing Fires	75
One Trouble With Stories	76
Stern	79
As Much Salvation As One Can Believe	82
Einstein's Violin	84
Renewal	88
Creed	92
How It Comes to Us	94
The Wings Below Our Hearts	95

About the Author

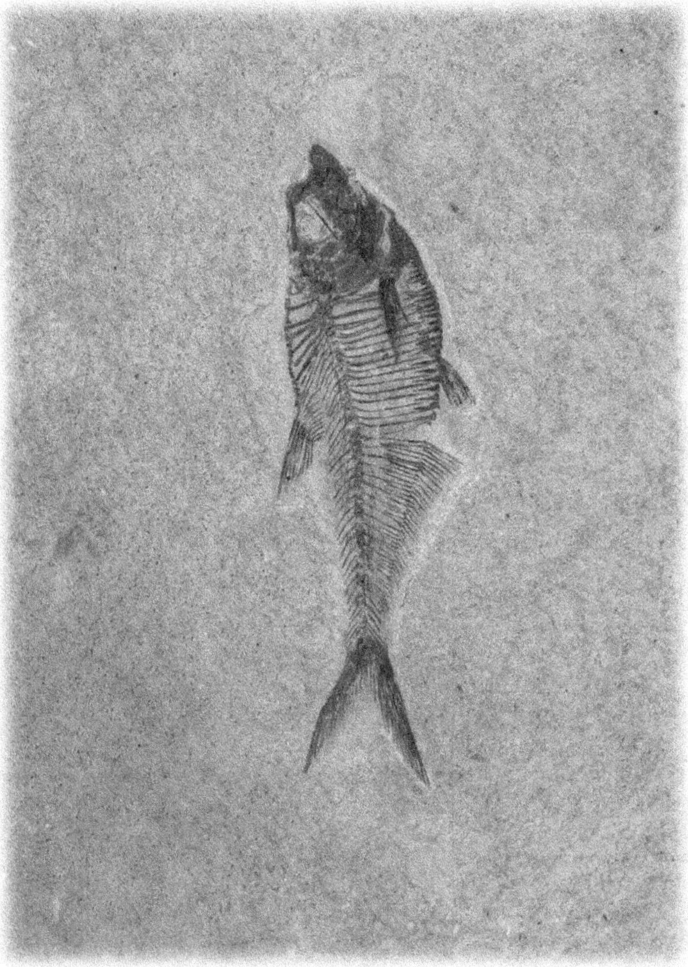

PART ONE

꙰

The Skeleton Parade

Old legend whispers them, bent-backed, crook-kneed from the nest
                of their military graves
in the low-ground cemetery by the river. They hobble a clacking
                cadence whose time
no mortal can count as they parade the lip, fleshless sentries assigned
to the eternal waters,

parody of the military formations they once were. They vanish
from sight at the instant one believes
they are visible. I knew some who lived near that river, who ventured
                in search of their parade
in the hours when churches lock their doors. And some tell stories
                of uncles who still carried wars,

who visited places where there are festivals for the dead. Each family
                cooks the best feast
it can afford, welcomes anyone who comes to the door. Later
                there is drinking and dancing in streets
crowded with bodies. But the dead have their own music and march
                only once a year.

Their dance is tied to a calendar we can't read. So no one sees them on
                the proper night, allowing
the story another year to age. And those who have left youth behind
                stay away knowing soon enough they will

join that procession and walk on bones softened with mud, gone
                weak between the unsure and unseen.

Shine

For Roy Bentley

With a cat burglar's caution, I sniffed
before tipping the jar to my nervous mouth.
Tasteless, but for the scorch of its passage.
I took a deeper hit. "Careful," someone said.
A puff of blue flame, soft as a cloud, enveloped
my brain. This was devil whiskey, home-cooked sin,
made, preachers swore, in some deep crevice
of hell. I'd seen pictures of stills, secreted
in hollows, guarded by grim faced men with guns.
Here was the stuff of *Thunder Road,* a hundred
patchwork hillbilly jokes, the liquor that gave birth
to NASCAR. Above me, the moon wobbled
and throbbed. Moss curled dark tendrils between
my toes, fur growled along my spine.
The rank blessing of wood fires gathered around me.
Governments and laws collapsed to ruin,
perished in graveled embers. When the jar came
to me again, I was enlisted in an army
that would not pay taxes or pave roads.
I would live among fallen trees, bathe in the sand
of creek beds. There was no flag worthy
of my salute, nothing I needed to pray to.
A sorry morning awaited, but this close
to the clear waters of sin, I wanted nothing but
to link arms with the devil and dance
a clumsy sinner's two step under a moon
that would neither fall not hold still.

What the River Built

The river might have offered escape
        had it not run too quickly to allow
entrance into the brown swell.
        Below what we could see
lay rocks fractured to angles and blades,
        the mud of its belly folding over
thousands of arrowheads too flawed
        for flight, so drowned instead.
Without trying, the river built
        one more obstacle that made
a fortress of the town. Ronnie Gayden,
        who had kin buried in almost
every graveyard in the county,
        claimed an uncle or step-grandfather
drowned diving from the rail trestle
        into the river not long after
the dam was built. Another text
        for nightmares, a water harsh
as the God we were taught to fear.
        Like all deities, the river's threat
was endless, and still is
        for a boy eyeing the twists
and braids of current, figuring
        his weight against the water's spread.
I live close to lakes now, man-cut,
        deceptive islands of water.
In warm months, water takes back
        a few of us land-walkers,

releases them only when they are
>   more water than earth, one means
of escape from that almost-nameless town.
>   And we who lay burning with
the desire for other places found ways
>   over ancestors drowned by time
or legend, their bones gone
>   soft and milky in a universe
made finally of water.

The Conversions of the Body

Neither red-faced coaches
or willow-wristed counselors,
too young for their beards, too anxious
in their desire to reach us,
could explain how we change
as we fall into life,
how we transform into bodies
shaped for the journey ahead.

Uncertain of constellations
spinning in the gut, the assemblies
of stars, the lifetimes required
for a spaceship to reach
the far suburbs of the universe,
I held my questions. The body
was both stranger and universe
and the church of flesh was all

I would believe in.
I heard stories of quicksilver
conversions, bodies trembled
in white-hot ecstasy at
the very lip of heaven. But
I never witnessed it once. A friend
who rolled his truck and walked away
without spilling his beer decided

to stop driving. Not the expected
conversion, but all he had
just then. He died quiet as breath
sipping tea and reading e-mail,
his essence slipping into
the inconsistencies of the universe.
It's that essence ministers call for,
       the same essence I inhaled

       in the white noise of my knee
giving way to a careless blocker.
I vanished inside my breath.
The longer the pain held,
the longer I held the smoky center
of my being, the wounds

I would need to go forward. Say
we enter this borderless field
as energy and leave the same way,
our bodies and the lives they inhabit
vanishing into the shapeless
vowels of our final breath.

Reading By the Moon

Between crescent and half,
    the dull, pitted molar

of moon gnaws its corner
    of sky, throbbing to devour

night's dull bouquet
    of stars. Antique recipes

of galaxy and dust, flat reflections
    of sun, the source makes

no difference to an appetite
    never filled by its share.

Today the dentist showed me
    photographs of the falling

stone wall my teeth resemble,
    age-worn, carious. I've stepped

over and through such walls
    into graveyards where stones,

darked by moss, so time-blurred
    names and dates can be read

only by hand, make
    an anthology of the dead.

No light will resurrect
        the legends etched

into those leaning stones,
        stories gone silent as

the passage of hours.
        Those walls last years

longer than I will need
        teeth to allow me

the dignity of chewing
        my own meals. And after

my last meal or the one
        before it, I hope my eyes

hold enough light
        to see sun or moon

continue the cycle they made
        long before I arrived,

determined to know
        the names of all I saw.

The Book of Forgetting

By now she's tired of stories
        spotlighting her early deeds,
actions too endearing to be
        plotted, or the years before
she came, blanks of time distant
        as fires in the granite hills

west of us. Last week, a downturn
        in the atmosphere brought smoke
drifting raw currents only made
        visible by smoke's motion.
It trespassed flatland streets and yards.
        At bedtime, I whispered

her away from apocalypse
        and bad dreams, promised
clear skies, knowing my blood
        would pace sentry for hours
after neighbor lights went dead
        and the shrouded moon

took its perch in the sky.
        I know there is a book, more
than one, where the names
        of dead towns and their citizens
line the white pages neat
        as grave plots. We see

our place in that book once
        when we are born, once more
when we die. So I can't say
        the fate of anyone, of those
facing the flames, whether
        they weep or pray or howl

a fiddler's laugh. That's why
        I tell my daughter stories
we both know the ending of,
        so we can forget what truth
lies inside a book
        neither of us will read.

Ghost Stories With Knives

There were houses, their porches rotted as old teeth, windows dark as
 blood
in every town I ever lived in as a boy. Places where fathers had gone
 to work

and never returned. Streets where children had vanished, leaving only
 a shoe,
a math book abandoned on the curb. No trace of where they had gone.

We knew early that our lives would be short and confusing.
That there was no point in avoiding pain. So we were never surprised
 when

things went wrong, when the thin silk that held the world we knew in
 place
began to tear away. The boy who held a knife under my chin trembled

with an electricity he could not name or control. My biggest fear
should have been
 his fear.
One Christmas the children's choir went caroling at a house
 where

I'd heard a family was found seated for dinner, their heads chopped
 off
and piled on the table. The knife was pocketed. I made it home
 without blood.

The ghosts and nameless killers, the boys who equate sharp things

with fear,
still roam the suburbs of foreclosure, camp in houses with no curtains.

Rusty nails are still sharp. Broken glass still longs to pull blood from
   bare feet.
The world's sharp edges still push at shadows, still sing the dumb
   spells cast

by children. Adult-sized, we wrestle other fears. They are endless
and we have a name for each one. No one ever knows the name of the
   child

gone missing, the family slaughtered. They are shadows, as far from
   us
as the trembling boy with the knife is from me right now.

What We Are Coming To

The first thing waiting is a list
of all your misdeeds, the lies
repeated, the small treasures
pocketed, each one drawn in
a calligraphy that makes
the tiny sin more significant
than it seemed in life. You read
the list aloud, then compose
apologies for each one.

After this you find
every animal, every small creature
you killed—each deer or dog,
every mosquito slaughtered by
a lazy slap, every fish pulled
from a pond or swift creek.
You will have to bury
each of these and make
amends for their careless demise.

Next is reserved for addicts, which is
all of you who say you aren't.
Here are all the substances
you took in—the powders, the bags
of leafy weed, the wading pools
of Old Crow, vodka and schnapps.
Now you pour all those bottles,
pitch all those vials and bags
into the clear and endless river.

Somewhere in all the labor,
in the digging, the singing
of apologies, pitching away all
that nearly pitched you, you find
nothing you do will change
any wrong or kindness you've done.
The life you lived is all
you can leave behind.
Now eternity can begin.

The Jesus Year

What in this school yard, where the power saw whine
of kid noise splits open an afternoon gone electric
and rank with spring, reminds me

you would be almost 33 today? If you were ever born.
The Jesus year, my friends and I called it, as we saw it
rise before us, the careening of our twenties truly finished,

the near-calms of marriages and jobs that might last,
the notion of children, descending. And left behind,
the early wreckage. Including you. You and all the others

who arrived as fear and complication. Selfish, some say,
and I would not argue. Murder, others claim,
and I will leave them to what they think. We were

poor and mad and scared and young, to quote Jack Butler.
The drugs didn't help. Or the anger ignited, not drowned,
by endless cans of Budweiser. There is more to say,

but I am not the one to say it. Back then I said
We'll do what you want. It's your choice. Knowing exactly
what the choice would be. Unable to imagine it being different.

Kid, you would not have had a chance. In that time, that place,
the only choice would be the one we made. It isn't often
the past resurrects so violently, tearing at errors I'd already excused.

And you, nameless, genderless, never more than
a shadow trying to pass its dark palm over our lives, arrive
on the cusp of your Jesus year, one more ghost

of my past visiting me in this life I could not conceive
thirty-three years ago, life where I often feel like a trespasser,
where I know part of my luck was in letting go of you.

Landscape Rising From Solitude

If you drive the country roads
around here, you will find old barns
holding fast against the gravity
of gentrification, their wood
worn gray as twilight, boards gone
like the teeth in a friend's mouth,
those absences that become
all you can see when he smiles.
Time's erosion leaves little
to smile about as nails loosen
their grip in wood's fabric.
Those structures were built
with the help of neighbors or men
hired for a few days' labor.
Once each of those nails gleamed
bright as a new moon.
There are a thousand parallels
for the empty bed, the house
devoured by silence. It takes
a while and a then a while longer
to live as though you are
your single tenant, to find
the narrative that is more than
a drone of loss. For weeks
after the slow crumbling
of my first marriage, I slept
on the couch, the television
she left behind dim accompaniment
to addled sleep. One night,
a story returned, shared

by a friend during his divorce.
A kinsman, too distant to own
a name, found himself expelled
from his house after decades
of blasphemy and hard drinking.
Across the road, he built
a madman's lean-to out of
limbs and scrap wood, any trash
that provided the illusion
of shelter. From there he could
rise from solitary hibernation
and harangue the woman
who had borne and raised his children,
then closed the door when
prayer provided no further comfort.
Drunk on home-brewed wine
or whiskey, he yelled his soul empty
at the house he nailed the roof on
and painted, that sat now,
complete in its silence.
Some days he stood in the road
to tell any who passed
of her perfidy. That story,
like his voice, is lost in wind
and mud, in the collapse
of his habitat. Now it dwells
only in the wordless humming
that sleeps in us, a near silence
roused only by trespass,
like the machine-whine of wasps
I nearly walked into once
as I explored a barn beginning

its fall. I backed out, stepping
into the solitude of my body.
And one night, inside the same body,
I found myself leaning
against the wall at a party,
a party so like others
I had no reason to speak.
Better to pull myself away
from the wall, find my coat, walk
to the house where the quiet paused
at my entrance, then stirred
like the sleep-drugged companion
who half-smiles and makes room
so you can at last lie down.

PART TWO

Animals Invented By Longing

It began with a neighbor asking
        if I could identify a print he found
                pressed into the soft mud around
his trash cans. Four-toed, broad as the palm

of my hand, this was not the track of any
        city-nervous deer or weasel cousin, no heart
                that would be satisfied by
picking our kitchen refuse. Twenty feet away,

another print, the same animal, but smaller.
        In the weedy scruff by my back fence,
                we found a final print, and beyond that
the cloven heart of a deer's hoof, evidence maybe,

of an impulse toward co-existence. Last night,
        I flipped on the flood light in time
                to find the red flicker of
a fox vanishing inside the dark. A few nights later,

I faced the startled yowl of a possum. From within
        the crumbled borders of their world,
                animals bear their identities and appetites
into ours. And neither of us finds room to shift

our desires or expectations for the other. So they flee
        and ignore me until the night when I go
                among my back yard's sparse trees
to lie down and let them see what has fallen.

The Beasts That Vanish

For Daniel Corrie

It was at one of those carnivals
        worked into extinction now, where

I saw the sign for a bear that would wrestle
        all comers, with a hundred dollar bill

for the one who lasted three minutes.
        My father pulled me past that tent

the way, ten years later, I saw parents steer
        their kids past the barker bidding

the men on the midway to come in and see
        the dancers. Behind him strippers

too young to know better or too tired to care
        crossed the little cat walk in front

of his tent. Those carnivals are memory now,
        hibernating in broken trailers and stories

of things that have turned into time's fossils.
        I wanted to see my father wrestle the bear, claim

the hundred dollars. I wanted to see the geek
        eat a live chicken. I believed the drawing of the bear,

its four inch fangs, claws like a fist
        filled with knives, rearing like a heavyweight

set to bench press the continent. I turned
        from the strippers' tent to walk

the midway, that trickster's alley
        whose one currency is illusion.

        *   *   *

A late night documentary about Bigfoot asks
        if the creature is our collective invention

or a cousin lost on an evolutionary shelf. Each video
        dissolves into grainy light after

a few seconds or is taken from too great a distance
        to say what creatures we are watching.

Even the narrators of some videos express doubt
        about the shy creatures they've shot. More than once,

I've considered what it would take to vanish
        into the wide-set maw of this country.

And some have shrugged off the past, dressed themselves
        in a new identity. It can become habit:

a community college president left Maryland
        and surfaced a few years later

in an El Paso bar. Discovered, he went back
        to teaching until the itch returned

and he vanished again, crossing a line
        from curiosity into myth, a creature

no one could explain or catch.

        *   *   *

There are night paths we feel but can't follow
        with our eyes, where each step becomes

a hazard, deliberation over whether a step
        or snare awaits, a steel trap set for

some predator, perhaps the beast
        you sense moving parallel and unseen

with you. In such dark, I could be
        anything, but not the animal

who knows the unfamiliar well enough
        to find a set of footprints and follows it

along the ridge time has cut, down
        into a past capable of birthing

creatures wise enough to vanish
        at our approach. They know

the narrow crevices that keep them safe
        until they decide to walk forward

within the shaking sights of man.

        *   *   *

The bear my father and I finally saw
        did not wrestle, but sat

on a flat trailer, one leg shackled,
        tethered by iron links theatrical

in their size. Around the cuff I saw
        flesh rubbed raw, fur matted

and worn away. The bear was muzzled
        though he seemed more apt

to lick a hand than bite it. For the price
        of a chocolate Yoo Hoo you could watch

the bear take the bottle between two paws
        and swallow, his single trick.

A child in the fog-belted mountains of Tennessee,
        his head stuffed with myths

of Davy Crockett and trappers, could ignore
        the slow rain, the butt-heavy slump

of the bear. Somewhere under stars wiped
    clear of prophecy, a bear and her cubs

prowled unleavened dark. A hunter perched
    in a tree, half-slumbering

toward first light. And when that bear sat straight,
    a growl low in his prehistoric throat,

I was glad for the muzzle, the links
    that held him. Glad for the distance

of rumored creatures who walk their trackless path
    through the heart of time, trailing a scent

that kindles growls from those able to see.

    *   *   *

In a few million years, the beings
    we will become, with their narrow fingers

and large heads, skin soft from rarely stepping
    into the half-toxic rays of sun,

may trade sightings of our kind, claim
    a few of us slipped through time unchanged

to walk as if earth had never changed and we could
    cast shadows wherever we please.

Night Deer

At night, deer the color of fog
drift on the slow-bending hills

behind my house. Their eyes, green,
luminous, shine against

whatever light reaches them.
If there is another world,

it is this one, filled
with creatures whose bodies

we can't touch, who resist
all our sweet lures. They know

where they are and remain
while we, less sure, call

after the promise of difference
that dangles from every new life.

Judas Lightning

Inlanders, we crouch, waiting for a hurricane,
                                          fill slow time
between approach and seizure counting batteries, stacking cans,
the preparations we still can make.
                                  The air smothers
with small rain. Soft thunder ripples the sky.
The swift kiss of lightning coils behind each cloud,
its devastations muted for now though it might come
in half the time a heart takes
                              to make one beat.

We see it as betrayal. Violation of the small commandments
we believe necessary
                to keep us protected
on this earth.
                Weatherpeople, the same ones
clogging my television to pass every blink
and hiccup of the hurricane,
                        tell us our chances
of being struck by lightning are the same as the odds
of winning the lottery.
                    So why do I know two people
who have survived blows from lightning
but no one who has won the lottery?

In a car with a dragging muffler,
                                     I gripped the dash
for sweet life as the brakeless vehicle spun
on ice-glazed asphalt. Sparks kicked from
under the car in great arcs.
    One spark, sucked
into the carburetor, would have turned us into a rolling
wedge of fire, or so we were told once the car stopped,
once we were all out and yelling at the driver,
at the fringe of onlookers, at the unblinking sky.

I've heard this hurricane's name so often
I know it like my own,
                       though once it has passed
into memory's cloud, it will blend into all
the other disasters
                 or near-disasters we've weathered.
Even at its worst, we trust the sky.
                           A few days
of good weather and we shine with forgiveness,
We even manage to accept,
                   if not forgive
the Judas kiss of lightning though the ones fallen
will not resurrect
             to show their scars,
marks of passage from one world to another.

The Bird Born Out of Weather

This sloppy mix, rain mingling with wet snow, dropped
all afternoon and into dark, sealing doors, silencing birds,

those little scraps of God or perhaps the disintegrating ego
of God. So in the morning, mud, no sound but water

dropping from limbs and eaves, a car down the street
revving to test the ice-skinned roads. By noon, roads will clear,

sun might even patch the ground. And a few sullen birds
will peck the soggy ground for what they can find.

But now, sleep dangles like the elusive silver bird
a boy from a story sees while out hunting one day

and chases until he has spent all his arrows, trying
to bring it down, until he is miles from any land

he knows, as far from sleep as the percussions of rain
and my own reckless brain have taken me. A story might

take years and this boy will be swept in a tumult of events
like a car spinning on black ice. He will travel for years

away from the valley of his birth, until a toss of fate
returns him to the place he started, a place still known,

but changed. The few who recall his name know him
as a tale to caution children from wandering too far,

not this stranger marked by travel and foreign battles
who throws a near-stranger's shadow over lanes settled

and made different over the years. And though he knows
five languages and a thousand names for God, he walks

to the edge of the settlement, listening again for the silver bird
whose song he followed into the life that became his own.

Dream's Animals

While we sleep, some portion
        of the body departs, shadowless.
It will not whisper
        of its travels when it returns,
but I have sensed its leaving
        in the kick of small muscles when
the one beside me enters sleep.
        And I have lain beside the sleeper
more nights than one, envying
        the wanderings of that small portion
of the soul, animal-shaped
        and alert, its landscapes
of bent trees, of grass broom-fry
        and itchy, mud underlying
each season in its turn. And I've stood
        to study what lies outside
my night windows though there is nothing
        out there for me to read, no words
to translate. What lives out there
        lives in the mystery of sleep, which is
the mystery the body holds.
        It is not salvation
our sleep animals offer, but escape
        from this present of star formations
and weather. And they will be gone
        when we wake to the few seconds
of amnesia before our lives rush
        to fill us again, dividing us
from the animals we have been.

Storms That Make Their Own Names

The crape myrtle's bark is peeling,
                                        long brown strips
disposable as old wrapping paper. We are deep within
the chapter of summer that promises rain every day
but rarely delivers.
                        Hurricane season is taking shape
in the ocean, storms brewing a blend
of wind and tide.

                      *   *   *

A friend once wrote me a letter—in the pre-computer days
when letters and long-distance calls were the only way
to stay in touch with anyone—
                                in which his architect's
hand sketched
a diagram of how hurricanes swirl to life.
                                                The rest
of the letter was about a New Year's Eve that I missed,
which included a drunk visit to my ex-wife's house
and an all-night bar.
                        There was also a section, not related
to New Year's, about seeing Faron Young and John Hartford
playing a concert on a riverboat stage.
                              I still find that letter,
folded in the pages of one book or another, always
a different book. The letter ended with a warning that
I could never be a scholar unless I read
every word Mark Twain ever wrote.

        *   *   *

This is the season of snakes

                taking siestas on back steps;
the air whines with bugs. My ankles jewel
with mosquito bites, little crests of dried blood.

I wipe my brow, say again

                we need
to get in the car and drive though there is
no place of real refuge.

                We could unfold fifteen maps
before we find weather cool enough to abide.
And once we were there, the only thing to do
would be to turn around and come back home.

        *   *   *

My friend died a few years ago,

                more than twenty years
after writing that letter to me. I barely recognized
the barbered man in his obituary. But the official record
never says

        what we know of friends: the dishes that began
with recipes and evolved into improvisations,

                the litany
of nearly-nameless bands he loved. The night he swept us
out the door like a storm still making a name for itself,
insisting

        we go on a post-midnight canoe ride.
It was going to rain, we said. There was work

the next day.
                "This will add twenty years
to your life," he insisted.

        *   *   *

The weather channel displays three storms,
two deep in the Carribean, one lingering south of Florida,
only one worthy of a name yet.
                I should go out
and rake up the crape myrtle's curved bark.
This fall, its flowers will fall
                so their juices stain
the sidewalk, tiny hearts washed loose of color. Odds are—
a gambler's guess—that two of the storms will blow
into nothing. The third might
                skirt land and vanish into
the great empty or make a hard turn inland.
It's always too soon to tell.

        *   *   *

There are weathers we have no refuge from.
                We all carry
what will not be escaped. Sentences brash
as a steamboat whistle announce us. An untasted spice
sinks through layers of stew.
                And one wide-awake soul
sees the moon and calls, "Let's add twenty"
to companions who push into moon-stroked waters
where those years are waiting.

PART THREE

Leaves

Full winter here. Fields frost-rough,
        stippled with mud. In two months,
tractors will churn mud, cutting rows
        for new plants.
               Two months after that,
pale green tobacco leaves, sticky with tar
        will open like wings, as they will
each spring in this state,
               a season's work
for the underaged and undocumented.

Two weeks after my family moved
        to North Carolina, I drove through
the brown heart of downtown Durham
        wondering why the air smelled like
a pack of fresh-opened Camels.
               Then the signs
on the red-brick factories, Ligget and Myers,
        Philip Morris, American Tobacco, where
the processed leaves were spun in paper cylinders
        to become Larks, Pall Malls, Lucky Strikes.

It's been a few years
               since I opened an envelope
thick with news and poems from Walter,
                        one
of my last friends who believed in letters.
        I'd pull the leaves of paper apart
                      and with each one,
the smell of smoke, sign that he had not

        quit the coffin nails, as my father used to say,
lighting up another one.

I have a brother who claims he will never live
        north of the Liggett Myers sign in Richmond.
Sometimes I wonder if I ever chose where to live.
        I moved back here for a year
                and thirty years
went by.
I got through the years in bars without ever
        taking up cigarettes,
                but I roll the windows down
whenever I drive through downtown Durham.

Now Durham, like the town where I live,
                like
        towns everywhere is scrubbed clean,
the little bars, the grills with C sanitation ratings
        gone now for glass front restaurants,
bars that only sell agave tequila.
                The cigarette factories
        are offices and lofts now,
and no one says what it took to erase the odor
        of raw tobacco, a smell I heard a farmer call
"money" as he stroked leaves, silky from curing.
                Then
        he lit a cigarette and coughed his lungs clear.

Exchange

Maybe it's like this: you're driving through
the weight of one more uneventful day,
the soft muscles of your back aching
when you see the man you might have been
loading tools into a pickup truck.

For a moment your eyes lock. A shock
passes between you. You see the house
where he lives, smell the food cooking there,
know which record he'll play when
he gets home, hear the words he says

before he goes out to work on the chest
he's building for his wife. Tonight he'll sand
the cedar top, the motion of his hand
erasing work cramps, the friends who left
and didn't return, the two years in prison.

Sometimes you fall prey to dreams of a life
you might have had. You recall the phone
ringing deep in the night, your friends begging
for you to come get them, take them away
from their hiding place near the phone booth.

Two miles away, a stolen car burned
in a thicket of trees. The road alarmed you
with its emptiness. You felt the power
and impatience of one who has performed
too many rescues as you slowed near

the smeared glow of the phone booth.
Your friends appeared from a skirt of trees, yelling
for you to drive. You waited for the explosion
of lights in your mirror. Later, those friends you wanted
to never see again gone, you drive home the long way

so you could see the wreck. One cop still sat,
his light waving lonely blue wings in the dark.
A tow truck had hauled the fire-blacked car husk
from the trees. You kept going, blue lights shrinking,
into the next life you could find.

Playlist for a Photograph of a Record Burning

                              August 16, 1966

Only one boy looks full on
at the camera, his glare
scorching the glass lens, a challenge
to all the years to come.
The others stare, as they should,
raptured, into the barrel where
cardboard sleeves curl into ash,
leave the slower melt of vinyl.
A voice rises, calling
for more lighter fluid.

"Hot town, summer in the city,"
sings the radio and that heat
flowers and grows around those
closest to the barrel. This heat,
the ministers promise, is nothing
beside the fires of hell.
In the next years, some children
congregated here will fight in
or protest a war, hear Hendrix
beg to stand next to their fire,
to marry the wrong boy or girl
or the right one, and enter
their own individual hells.

First the records, then
the Beatles wigs and dolls,
the magazines, lunchboxes,
a plastic guitar branded
with their faces, smiles that held
even as the plastic stretched
and folded into ribbons
of toxic smoke. Then,
other records: The Animals,
Stones, Kinks, Sonny and Cher
all fuel for the righteous flame.

"Love is a burning thing,"
warns Johnny Cash, though
his records are not the ones
burning here. But someone
loved those records once,
enough to save dollars earned
babysitting or cutting grass,
enough to count them out
one by one to pay for what burns now
as though music could
be unheard. More lighter fluid

and the boy still stares,
transfixed in the eye
of the camera. A year
or two and he will hear
Arthur Brown sing, "I am
the god of hellfire," and wonder
if fire ever truly bought
salvation. Ahead of him,
just under the ashes wait
moon landings, Nixon, Watergate,
glam rock, cocaine, Woodstock,
weapons of mass destruction,
disco, recession. He will learn
there is never enough fire.

Ellipsis

The lash-thin clouds dwindling above
        a line of trees no longer shaved
by winter's blade, but leafed in full
        spring array, remind me how many
spoken sentences trail into silence,
        hoping quiet can finish saying
what words did not.

The ellipsis at the end
        of the sentence spins outward
to the infinite, like dashes
        Emily Dickinson used to closer
her lines, little echoes
        of the unsayable that all poems try
to say.
        The first time I went fishing
        was like that, the unsure sidearm
of my cast unraveling above
        the solemn listening of water.

We were casting, as far as I knew,
        for flashes of light, lightning drops
in the water
        and we pulled back
        bare hooks that said all
I would ever know about fish
        and water.

                        We know how
sentences should behave, bending
            to points as fine and inevitable
as blades or fish hooks, their danger
            hovering just where steel stops.

Philosophers believe the eighty pound
            test line of their syllables will
reel in whatever whale
            of Big Thought they conceive,
one reason they stack words on top
            of words, believing there is language
perfectly matched to each thought.
            But for most of us, language will always
be the brother-in-law who got drunk
            and fell in the water the only time
the two of you went fishing,
                                    the one
            who borrows tools he doesn't return,
whose wallet is always at home
            when it's time to pay for dinner.

Small wonder some prefer
            to translate the long trails
silence makes, like contrails
            a jet draws against the empty
paper of sky,
                        a rain drop rolling
            down a gray panel of window glass,
spending itself as it moves.
            And rain returns us to the beginning,
to clouds, puffy breath-shaped poets

       who float without breath or anchor,
a grammar so endless and difficult
       we have only shapes, wordless stretches
to map the place
       all sentences move toward.

Source

Out of sore feet, out of roadsides sooted with dusk,
    out of gravel, jeweled crumbs of shattered glass, out

of the wide gesture of the hand toward heaven, out of
    the black trace of fire smoke over a chimney, wind shifting

its hips like a dancer, out of a thorn in a bird's throat,
    the body of a lark split open and baked, a coil

of blood coloring its bed of lettuce, out of the boundaries
of breath, come words.
                   And out of words, spells:

spells for a burned tongue, for healing the soft meat
of the foot after a splinter knifes into it.

Spell for a night's sleep and safe waking. Spell for
    the singed wax odor of a candle pinched dark,

a tiny core of flame jeweling the curling wick.
    There is the spell for reading, for making

an unruly child rest, for making medicine
    take hold, for fickle love and binding discomfort

for a heartless swain. A spell for wind
    tugging the fine top grains of soil,

a little wave migrating through the fence where
    nails work their way out of sour wood. The spell

to summon a certain god or to call all the gods from
    their wine presses. And out of those spells,

praise cries, screams, whistles carved bare as quarries,
    dredged empty of lime, abandoned hollowed bones.

And out of those spells, the rare voice that turns to singing
    in service to the things we stared at until

we knew them and what they should be named.

PART FOUR

॰৶

When We Burned the Diaries

It was the year of marriages ending,
the year of subjective truth.

It was the year we began to know
longing the way ash understands

flame, not with hunger for
bright consumption, but slow desire

to be again what was altered.
Crows, starved for sour meat,

flew from the bent limbs of trees,
sky a pulpit for their single notes

until that song staled. In light,
threads of green, of reds and dusty gold

shimmered in dusty wings
as though they might have dipped

into the fires our words made
and ascended, trailing inky smoke,

singing each one of our rank sins
until they were ash gone cold,

good only to dirty the hands
we soiled long before.

Shooting Pool in the Mental Hospital

Because memory is not the hovering bank shot that stops at the lip
    of the pocket and will not fall,
but the scatter of balls when the cue ball strikes, rolling
    hurried and random as roaches

scrabbling for cover in the just-lit kitchen of a greasy spoon, it's hard
    to say how we will read what lies there
once everything settles. The same memory that once struck mirth
    might flame in unexpected sorrow,

like walking again into the roadside chicken joint the night before
    Thanksgiving, 1977.
As soon as we walked in, a woman behind the counter began to scream
    that only queers and junkies

came in there and she was sick of it. She slammed into the back, the door
swinging
    in her wake and did not come back
though we could hear her yelling. A girl who wouldn't look at us brought
our chicken
    and we drove on,

wondering through full mouths what could have triggered her rage.
    The night before,
loaded on mescaline, it had taken us an hour to shoot one rack of balls
    from the table.

Everywhere we looked, impossible angles, endless sprawl of green
    possibility, the way
things should look when you are nineteen and unable to see beyond
    the next hour.

Our bad shooting and laughter began to draw dark looks from men betting
    money and pride, both
scarce in a town bitten in half by recession. And in two months
    I'd seen the owner and his son

beat customers so thoroughly ambulances were called. One of us scratched
    the eight ball and we left
for a place quieter and darker, somewhere our madness could find a corner
    and hide.

          *   *   *

Years later, that same friend, by now a believer in the enlightenment
    suffering could bring,
was ambushed by a mix of blood and rogue neurons, and the world
    became his church,

all matter mantled in light that fell slow and rich, like a painting
    of light. Everywhere he looked
waited a new place to worship, a new soul to bless. Such ecstasy will not
    walk free long.

A few nights after I saw him praying on a church's front lawn,
    he was delivered
to a hospital and his pacing brain was slowed by drugs whose names
    rang like gods of a faith

I'd never heard of before. When we were allowed to visit—this was
    a charter hospital, not a lockdown facility—
my then-wife and I drove out to see him. I tried
    not to taste the fear

I've always had of not being allowed to leave such places, the staff

       and patients reading
what I would not say, shuttling me off to rooms where I would spend days
       yelling for someone

to listen. But we sat a while in the cafeteria, then walked halls so calm
       I almost forgot
the misdirection bubbling under my heart. In the rec room, my friend suggested
       we shoot pool for a new car.

The sticks were warped to parentheses, and the twelve ball
       was missing, but we racked them up
while my wife played cards with a woman who spoke the whole time of
       her fear of devil-worshipers.

And there, in that place that housed the God-touched and the devil-frightened
       I shot the best pool I ever have,
the madness of those rooms conspiring with my body to bring me some touch
       of earthly if not divine grace.

          *   *   *

There are no martyrs in pool halls. Or standing over boiling pits
       of grease in chicken joints.
Sooner or later, the cost of what you sign up for becomes clear.
       And neither rage nor madness helps.

And if you had looked into the room that day and saw two men
        shooting pool
for imagined stakes, could you have said which was believed to
be mad and which could pass for sane?

Dice, Scripture, and Lost Winnings: An Unfinished Portrait

In one self-portrait, he sleeps, the pair of dice near his hand
    shining snake eyes. In another self-portrait,

a Bible thick as his pillow rests by his head.
    It's not clear which was painted first, but faith

has always been at least as much of a gamble as
    as betting your money on the fall

of the dice. There are the blind serpents of luck
    and players who know how to take the chance

out of any bet. And worse. In *Studs Lonigan,* Davey Cohen,
    exiled from Chicago, puts his last two bucks

in a craps game. The dice get hot for him
    and he leaves the game, trying to believe his luck.

The man who drew himself sleeping did not read
    that book. He believed the angles of the form,

the restorative power of sleep. Trusted the power
    of seeing ourselves to make ourselves new.

Davey Cohen is beaten, rolled, and abandoned, worse off
    than when he entered the game. Some might say

his winnings were those blind moments of hope
    when he supposed he'd eat a good meal, buy

a new suit, return home in style. The artist succumbed
     to the snakes of madness and died young, the tale

of his death filled with shade and unconnected lines.
     His winnings must be ours as well, the paintings

we stand before and try to absorb
     with a gaze unblinking as a snake's.

Pumpkin Spice and the Infinite Horizon Blues

Brown-shoed, seated in straight rows, we were taught
and believed the impossibility of measuring the horizon.

Today, waiting in line for coffee, the horizon seems as good
a goal as any, especially when a latte order goes

into greater detail than the directions Columbus had
when he cast off on what promised to be a new route

to the West Indies. Of course, he never got there. And customers
want no discoveries in their morning drinks. In front of me,

two women talk about the return of pumpkin spice as though
it was a ship returned after three years' absence, its hold filled

with spices enough to flavor endless meals, silks to clothe
a succession of queens and, most important, to make the captain

endlessly rich. What we knew of endlessness was the flat hour
before school ended, leaving us to navigate the slow walk home.

I don't recall when pumpkin spice bloomed into a flavor
that spread over late autumn like a cloud, but I know it was not

one of the spices Columbus hoped to fill the hold of his ship with.
Columbus never found the riches he thought should be his

by right of invasion, sat chained and coughing for six weeks
in a Spanish jail at the end of his New World adventure, even

his theory about the shape of the earth fallen into disrepute.
The narrow view of the horizon available as I walked home

or stared slow and wide out the window said
our boundaries were defined, a pencil slash along

the edge of a yardstick. Venture far enough from shore
and the horizon grows until it surrounds you, a tilting

indifference you notice gradually, then realize you must pursue
until the pursuit becomes like an obsession with riches, a piece

of music that demands to be heard over and over. In front of me,
a woman orders a soy latte, skinny, half-caf with extra foam

and a splash of something. Each year I drift a few knots further
from the shore where my students stand. I sip my plain coffee,

black, and recall that when I started teaching a joke about Nixon
fetched laughs. Now their brows furrow if I mention Dick Cheney.

The sooner they can silence my arcane concerns, the sooner
they can return to cell phones and pumpkin spiced coffee that turns

their eyes dewy with sugar. It takes a while to see how a journey can
slip off course and longer to understand that drifting off course is

the true purpose of journeys, especially when the horizon moves
so the distance between us is constant and as impossible

to measure as the weight of steam rising damp
from this cup and all the cups before it.

Counting Stock

I knew how to count, so
        it looked like an easy day's work
taking inventory in a store owned
        by the family of a friend, one
of the six or seven they owned
        in a string of small towns, stores
where you could find
                shoelaces, shotgun shells,
dishes and headache powders, all
        nestled in a few well-planned aisles.
All we had to do was count
        what sat on the shelves.
We knew the numbers we wrote down
        were impermanent as the rain
sliding down the plate glass windows:
        tomorrow, winter hats would sell,
new supplies of cereal and T shirts
        would be sorted on the shelves.

Two-thirds of a life since then,
        and if you had asked
what I thought I'd be doing
        today, I could not have mapped
any of the steps that made
        the boy I was then, the one
volunteering to take the trash out
        so he could smoke a bowl, into
whoever I am tonight.

                      In a swamp
          two hours from where that store stood,
scientists have discovered a band
          of swamp cypress older than Jesus.
Some items resist inventory.
          Christmas had just slipped by,
and December's dusk dropped quick
          and silent as the rain that wrapped us
each time we stepped outside, making
          the matches in my pocket so hard
to strike I considered buying
          a lighter from the store.
Our hours translated into cash,
          erasing every number I'd written down,
but that night I could not stop counting
          whatever came before me.

Today it's hard to count
          or even separate the clouds scooting
low and dark over the treeline,
          choked with their deliveries
of rain. I have watched more afternoons
          of rain than I will ever count, spent
too many hours believing I might
          reach some plateau of knowledge
described by poets and priests. Now,

    I only want to mark one more slash
on some imaginary slate where
    some unseen scorekeeper keeps tracks
of what counts in this life.
    One more mark. And then another one.
Even after the counting stops.
                      One more.

Lottery Tickets and the Odds of Retirement: A Meditation

Now night's little rain
comes gentle as the green
of seasons not yet arrived,
silent as the gray that claims
each bristle in my beard.
I woke to the tapping
brushes of water, pulled into
my post-sleep musings
on the crumbling republic.
Given that I have less
to worry about than
the middle-aged former welder
who worked to join
thesis statement and body paragraph
in the Wednesday night
purgatory of my class,
a hurdle he had to cross before
he could learn programming,
or the printer who went to work
to find the shop closed and had to
choose between nursing
and culinary arts, I should
close my book, try again
for sleep. Instead of counting
sheep or raindrops, I could
try to number the days until
retirement. Still too many
to calculate. And since I lack
the gambler's poise and seldom
buy lottery tickets, since

there are no bricks of gold
nesting in the roots
of the family tree, work,
as Guy Clark sang, will be
my middle name. For
a while longer. But I can last
a few more years if the flock
of yellow birds that swarmed
the tree outside my office
last spring returns to tell me
this moment is all
the life we have or need to have.
Random sights, like the wire-
perched bluebird I saw
yesterday, the little tongues
of crocuses splitting
cold dirt remind me how odd
and wonderful it is
to live in a place where
bluebirds appear in February.
So maybe it won't seem so long
until I'm driving home from
my last day, my chest opening
like an accordion filled with sky
as I name the philosophers—
Wittgenstein, Kant—I can read
now that I have time.
Schopenhauer. The symphonies
I will finally absorb. But
the next morning, I will probably
sleep late, read one more
thin book of poems or a thriller

from the used book store,
listening to records I've played
so long I barely hear them.
But on the ride home, cruising
a universe adept at the bait
and switch, the three card monte,
I might forget I've spent
four decades saving for poverty.
So I might stop and spend
the ones in my pocket for
a few lottery tickets,
my share of the gambler's dream,
the turn for the better
my students work for.
In the silence of my car,
I'll scratch away the silver
facing, whole and electric
in that moment, each breath
a summons to the hope
that still brings me
to the work each day requires.

PART FIVE

The Night of Changing Fires

On the far side of this continent, houses are drowning
in fire,
        even small towns left skeletal, timbers
and unburned brick and metal. Tonight, I feel
electricity, low as the murmur of flame under
a gas log,
        buzzing deep in my blood, forcing
my eyes to open each time they close.
                So many things
encompassed in that single word *fire:*
                warmth,
destruction, the beginning and end of time.
Tonight if I stepped outside
                I could make myself believe
the edges of plants in our yard, the spears of grass
are outlined in fire, their mantles of flame
gleaming without smoke or heat.
                If I switch on
the 24 hour news, I could wait through the harvest
of lying politicians, the celebrity scandal du jour,
and hear
        which direction the fires are turning
and wonder again how long I will have been sleeping
when the flames turn in my direction.

One Trouble With Stories

The biggest house in town and we were the lucky
sons of bitches building it. "Someday you'll show this place
to your kids and tell them you built it," the owner told us.

He loved to sit in the shade and watch us, a folder of papers
ignored on his lap. After a while, the drinks he mixed from
the cooler in his trunk kicked in and he would talk

to anyone not busy enough to fend him off. Redwood planks
for the flooring, cut to order, were coming from California.
Marble countertops from Italy. He was going to dig a pool

big enough to float a ship. He pointed where it would go
though his finger found a new location every afternoon.
Comeuppance for all the bastards in this town who tried

to make sure he would never have a pot to piss in. He waved
as if erasing the just-visible rooftops of the town
most of us called home, who came up the hill each morning

carrying Cokes, coffee, hangovers, the weight of the hours
waiting for us. Once he moved in, he said, he would
walk out the front door every morning—the door that was

already delivered, waiting in the trailer with everything else
it wasn't time to install yet—and he'd look at that town
full of assholes and sons of bitches and he'd take a leak

and, by God, hope they could see him. We framed the walls,
tacked up sheathing, hammered plywood for the roof when
he retreated again to the shade or took a drive down the hill

into that town of tightwad bastards. Plumbers and electricians
arrived to flesh out this multi-storied monument to
one man's skill at holding a grudge. He was in Reno, went

the story I heard more than once, down to his last couple of dollars,
and he dropped a token in a slot machine. It spit out
a jackpot, enough for a seat at the poker table, and by dawn,

he was as rich as he'd ever been. He used the winnings
to build a business—none of us was sure what the business was—
and came back home to get even richer. "Trust your luck."

He raised his cup in a toast to his own luck. For us, luck
was a job that would last long enough to collect unemployment
through the winter. What we had after the check was cashed

barely paid for a few drinks, much less a night in a casino,
even if one could be uncovered in our Bible-belted state.
The windows were being installed, including a stained-glass

fantasia ornate enough for any cathedral, when
four black sedans rolled up the lane. Men in dark suits
put the owner in back of a car and left as silently as they'd come.

We looked around, wondering what we should do.
The next day we were sent to another job. The owner never
came back as far as we knew. Windows got broken out,

the door kicked askew. I went there once, before it turned
to a complete ruin, one more unfinished thing in a world of
unfinished things.
                      And that is why I can tell you

it was not a house we built but an apartment complex.
And the one the cops came for was no home owner
but a foul-mouthed kid from Texas, his face scorched

from the sun. Two city cops carried him off,
not for pickpocketing bank accounts but for armed robbery,
assault, breaking and entering, the roster

of small caliber crimes. Twelve people watched it happen
and by quitting time, each one had repeated the story, changing it
a shade with each telling. Because, finally, facts matter less that

what you believe as you stand inside the story, waiting to tell it.

Stern

The first poem I heard him read—this was
on Bill Moyers' TV show about poetry—was "The Dancing"
about a family's unplanned twirl of ecstasy in the last year
of World War II, the three of them, young Stern
and his parents, not so young but younger, I'd bet, than I am
writing this, all dancing, the father using hand and armpit
to squeeze out farting sounds, the three of them
safe from and irreducibly caught in the wheel
of history. From here, the cities of the 40's seem
like benevolent wildernesses that now exist only in myth
where men in loose clothes stroll the boulevards, wearing
hats and ties and women wear pencil skirts, everyone
smoking. Jazz rolled from some windows, symphonies
shrouded darker windows. Bars were filled with shadows,
free of TV screens. Doors stood open because no one had
air conditioning yet. I taught Stern's poem for a few semesters
until two students, who enrolled thinking it would be
the easy A it was before I began teaching there, demonstrated
their arm fart technique for the class. This was at a school
for rich fuckups, many simply waiting for the trust fund
to begin paying off like a slot machine. But from them,
a few emerged to love poems for at least a year. Still,
"The Dancing" never made the pirouette back into the rotation.
If you teach, you know the drill—you learn which pieces
will teach something and lean on those until they have
no more to tell you, then find a few more. Or maybe
you choose a book or two each year and stumble through,
never sure if you've said anything worth saying.
Twenty-five years of five classes a semester and I've learned
which lessons I can trust. And my taste runs counter

to my students who are raptured by waterfalls, fields
of green frosted by Wordsworth's daffodils
while I try to explain the blossoming joys of decay,
of alleys through poor neighborhoods, the acne
of rust on a car left abandoned on the highway.
I never punched a clock in a coal or steel mill or I would sing
a spot for them in the pantheon as well. And the pantheon,
that endless, mythical anthology, is where
we all hoped to be going when we sat in workshops,
then later in bars, basking in some small triumph or nursing
wounds we would forget. It was the fall I got divorced
when a new professor handed back my poems and suggested
I read Gerald Stern, advice I put aside with a lot of other
good suggestions. It was a few years later, after school
was done, that I heard Bill Moyers talk to Stern
and went looking for his books. I was landscaping
in the day and teaching composition at night. Somewhere
I learned that he had spent years in community colleges,
a fact that fills me with joy when there are papers
to grade and poems that want to be written. The first time
I saw Stern was at a writers' conference as he moved
slow as a planet amid a constellation of smaller poets.
Heavy with mirth and awe, his face might have belonged
to the deli owner who rings up your Reuben. Or
the ring watcher telling you that the middleweight who keeps
dropping his left will never move up the card. Better dressed,
he might have been the lawyer drafting the Talmudic passages
making it possible to leave your estate to your fat dog
and not the grandkids who never visit or call. I'm old enough
to have outlasted some of the world's fascination
with youth. I can tell the students in my class, the Botoxed
ladies where I buy groceries that little runs

as wild as an old man's heart. Those fires are the ones
I need to keep this pen moving across the page.
Tonight, somewhere north of me, I hope Stern is writing
a poem. When I saw him read a few years ago,
we talked about community colleges and he signed
his book "Your fellow slave," though it's been years
since he was slave to any job. I left the reading,
grateful for the angels of poetry the ones who come
on half-sprained wings to bless all that rusts and ages,
who come to us when we are wild enough to dance.

As Much Salvation As One Can Believe

For George Looney

I should start this poem with a priest
pouring a shot of whiskey, but that would
make it one of your poems, not mine.
But now I've already begun, and I know
you could make believe an angel
sits in a chair opposite the priest.
So I will give you the priest and add fire
rolling in the hills over town, smoke
black as a cassock filling the sky.
Black at noon, blacker still at midnight,
thin seam of fire visible and moving
above them. There are no angels
and, for now, no fires where I live.
I will tell you it has rained enough today
to drown any angels or any good intentions.
It's hard to consider salvation if
your first thoughts are safety or food,
or if you are shaking for the shelter
of a drink of wine or whiskey.
Just as I imagined the priest.
The way we both imagine lives
and try to fit them into crude boats
of song, somewhere they can float
safe from fire, the water deep
and slow as the motion of wings.
The priest is tired of promising heaven
with no strings attached. The angel wants
to fall into flesh and live in the world
he once scorned, to search for

a woman he danced with
on his last mortal night, when
he was human and owned a future.
Outside the dance hall, he wrote her number
and bent to hug her. When he recalls
the soft possibility of their bodies,
the lemon and honey smell of her,
the motions of clouds, of prayers
the priest has lost, of fire all
vanished into the flood of memory
and that rises with it, all
the salvation we can believe.

Einstein's Violin

Music builds itself, somehow, on numbers,
                                              a house that rises
so naturally we forget it has architecture, a plan
that might be studied for years, but never mastered.
Years of practice and still the foundation might float
unanchored or the placement of fingers fail.
                                                       The small
improvisations that make an adventure of melody
might slide by unheard. You could
play for years without learning to recognize the swerve
into a chord that shifts the tune's field,
the way Einstein believed
                                      planets might alter the focus
of gravity. Physics, after all is built of numbers as well,
its long-limbed equations built to probe
the architectures of the universe.

Some know the bodies of instruments as well
                                                            as those
who spend their energy charting the heavens, watching for
new eruptions among constellations they know like the names
of their children. Last night, leaning against the stage,
I wondered if the guitar player saw the small brilliance
of Venus, the infinite measures
   encased in an instrument
when he tipped his head back, let his eyes roll shut
and let his fingers stir a cauldron of notes,
that blossomed, then faded
                                            into white noise that
   swallowed all that lay before it.

If the drummer or keyboard player
                                       missed a note,
time stumbled, then found its footing. Unlike gravity,
music is not shared equally.
                            There is no place I know
where gravity differs to any degree we can measure.
But it is possible to tell the good player from the not-so-good,
to read who is playing and who is phoning it in for the night.

For those who are scholars of nothing in particular,
one entertainment is watching those who know their business.
When one scientist's book makes its argument for
one construction of the universe
                                while his friend
argues for another way of coercing the same arrangement
of space and time,
                 I find some joy in knowing
there is no final answer,
                       the way two pianists might
make different tunes of "Stella by Starlight."

I've seen enough pictures of Einstein holding a violin
to wonder if anyone recorded

 his playing. A search
through the dustbins of the internet told me
there was a recording of Einstein playing
Mozart's Violin Sonata KV 378, but a little more reading
told me this recording was fake,
                           Einstein's playing attributed

to Carl Flesch. Without anything to hear
and only the testimony of his wife and friends,

                                            we are

left to wonder what constellations took shape while he played,
what new equations timed

                        the age

and velocity of those universes?

Did he conjure the humming between spheres
that is almost music?

                              Einstein would come

from his study, pick up the violin
or sit at the piano and play, his mind revolving
in the deep reaches of this universe or the next one.

I can look at a page of sheet music or math problems,
but read nothing,

                      but I know the sound of the music I love

when I hear it, even if its making remains as mysterious
as mathematics or the unreadable realms of stars.

Maybe all the universe is navigated

                            with numbers,

measures of the incorporeal waves that govern
time and space,

                    commanding that we age one-half breath

at a time. So each clock tick is both
a tallying up and a subtraction.

                            Even while your fingers

gain velocity over the keyboard, the instrument of the body
is pummeled by gravity, a pressure that remains
constant and uncounted.

We have all come awake
                        to a voice that stopped
just as our eyes opened, the secrets breathed away
the instant an eye registered light.
                                Sometimes
in that hovering where the body has
no particular beginning or end,
                              I'm struck by a line
ringing fire, and, for that moment, true as a chord.
Then I must decide whether to find a notebook
and write it down or believe it will linger
through my single journey of sleep.
                                    Last time I wrote,
"Slow lunch. Matches. Bring dolphins and worry," a
constellation
I will never navigate.
                        I retreated to the window,
where I counted a few houses still lit,
burning their way to or from the eternal dawn
where Einstein crafts a slow melody,
the start of a day's mysterious universe.

Renewal

We are driving through our laments for
    what this town has become, almost lost though we turn

routes so familiar I hardly need to steer. The clubs gutted
    to build shops and chain restaurants, the all-night diner

where I once drank coffee and watched the world shrink into light
    a condo now, the bowling alley beside campus a Target

where students can buy gym shorts and toilet paper, all these lead
    to a recital of what stood in each non-existent building

and remade space. Without speaking, we are steering out of town,
    along a two-lane road still robed in shade, trees pressed

close to the road's blunt shoulder, lower limbs bend groundward
    like animals come to drink at an oasis. Then

the road widens and light splashes the asphalt, the wall of trees
    broken to reveal a cut clear, still littered with tree trunks

lying askew, broken limbs dangling, casualties of the ongoing battle
    between space and commerce. And beyond, houses, all twinned

in their sameness. I slow the car. No evidence anyone lives here.
    No one mowing or pulling weeds from beds uniformly mulched

in pine bark. No kids shooting baskets or riding bikes. My brother and
    his ex- dwelled for a while on a similar street. I had to count

doors to find their place. The fourth one on the left. Or maybe the sixth. When I moved here, this road was barely paved, a path

through trees, its few houses hidden by pin oak and pines. A good place
    to lead an invisible life. Now, slashes of orange paint color

the ground, sign that this road is due to be widened, repaved. A decade
ago, when our daughter would only nap in the car, I would

  drive this road and a maze of others, circling the satellite towns of
      the county before the bosses began building glass towers

  that shine like new needles, even at might. Ground is broken, then come
    carpenters, masons, crane operators, craftsmen who will never

walk the rich carpets that will fill halls that exist only on paper now
    or "take a meeting" around tables as big as a front porch.

Then come computer jocks, software manipulators with their needs for
    Thai food, bike lanes, fair trade coffee. Now restaurants can

charge eighteen bucks for an appetizer. The bar where I got drunk for
    the last time is a lot loaded with earth movers now. Past the colony

of still-life houses, we see a mailbox, its top half crowned by the dome
    of a skull, the bottom adorned by jawbone, so opening the mailbox

offers the illusion of a skull yawning for reasons, both good and evil.
    In the side yard, a windmill, not built of angle iron, curved blades

dicing the wind, but something from a book a child reads, built of wood,
    its tiny windows leaded into diamond shapes. I'd call it

life-sized, but how many in recent years have seen such a thing?
    Let's say it was large enough for its job. Which, right now, is

pulling our attention from the road as we slow and then pull over,
    the car slanted on a shallow ditch bank, our bodies still as the street

we just passed. No matter how motionless our bones, time continues
    its slow walk forward, stubborn as a morning runner who knows

the limits of his aging legs but keeps his dogged pace. Time will roll over
    all our wishes for the past to hold. We need to breathe deeply enough

to appreciate the allotment of days we treat like the abandoned houses
    of our youth, places to be occupied, then destroyed. Denied

a last drink, I stood outside the loud bar, emptied, feeling the start that
would change. And keep changing. If this was a poem, if I was a wiser
    man,

I'd find some explanation for what it all means, lessons from a self-created
    Virgil or just myself in the guise of a man almost whole. But

I'm just a man sitting beside his wife, staring at something I'll never have
the patience or skill to make. Maybe once I would have bent close enough

to draw a brush over each plane of wood, coloring each one to contrast
    its neighbors, each an irreplaceable part of the whole. The lie bosses tell

workers until they falter. But the windmill, with its ability to snare the eye
    echoes a more cautious time, when painting a structure or sanding

a piece of wood correctly meant something. While we stare, the eyes in
the skull flash red, little hazard lights, a caution that someone is watching,

pulling us from what thickens in the capsule of our car: how easily we
have dreamed ourselves into this place, a paradise artificial

as the new structures we curse but can't stop from coming. We drive
away, accelerating back into our lives, returning to our porch where we see

cranes above the trees, busy at the rebuilding there is no end of.

Creed

Believe in fire and the dream of fire,
        in light both sky-woven and kindled
in hearths. Believe in the gems
        of street lights unraveling a carpet
home, the blink of windows suddenly dark,
        masking whatever violence or love
lies down in there. Believe the myth of life
        as a kind of burning, saints and lovers
consumed, gone to cinder, gone to ash.
        Believe in Prometheus, his eternal torture
for stealing fire, the fire I feel
        when I touch my child's forehead.
Now I believe the little prayers, warm
        as air, but unconsumed, as I drive
for juice, cough medicine, soup, anything
        that might damp the body's fire.
I've spent hours tending fires, staring
        into the red gravel and rubble
wood becomes as fire transforms it. This city
        in its cloak of cold fluorescence
denies that it was once a city of hearths,
        each house gathered around it pocket
of wood or coal. Before gas was harnessed
        or the coughing ignition of Model A's.
Before the spans of railroad ties, before
        all windows were glass. Tonight,
any late driver passing the shaded glow
        of my window won't know I'm waiting
for my daughter's fever to pass.
        They just know someone holds off sleep

the way someone in the first tribe
        to possess fire lay in the half-warmth
of the fire circle, sighted up the steeples
        of smoke at the stars whose fires
men will not touch, their heat
        dispersed across centuries of sky.

How It Comes To Us

First day of spring and a forecast
        for snow or freezing rain. The plants
too wise to have sprouted curl quiet
        under cold mud. Close to here, a boy dreams
of hitting baseballs in high arcs
        over a flawless green outfield. Somewhere
a man turns his car key, hears only
        dry grinding under the hood. We live
in a world of things determined
        to break promises: cars, little machines,
marriages. I could tell you about
        the repairman who just shook his head
and said, "Get a new TV." I have told stories
        of times weather was betrayal,
like the time your mother and I expected
        to wake to a morning bedded
under snow. But the ground was bare, the air
        iron-cold, giving me a day to work
in frozen mud, lashed with cold wind.
        Those days passed. The slow engine of spring
turns and we are briefly held in
        the perfection I began to believe in
the first time I saw you.

The Wings Below Our Hearts

Tangled in the gray sheets of waking,
        I barely register my first
conscious breath until the bird
        that sailed into my body to roost
half a life ago calls, bony wings
        battering the soft cage of my ribs
until I stand, groaning against
        my aging spine, count
the sunrises I did not rise for.
        As though I could raise my arms,
be claimed by the gods of flight,
        guided by vectors of horizon
and sun, earth a stubbled patchwork
        of brown and green, the cursive
of roads an unreadable message.
        Air in my beaked nose razors
through decades of city gunk
        as I rise into higher, thinner realms,
feel continents ready themselves
        for the chaos of descent.
And in the vacuum quiet of coming
        awake on earth, I hear
the quiet fluttering of the birds
        held deep in my wife's body,
hear again the little songs
        I heard the first time
I leaned close to her, whispers
        promising that if I listened
I would learn the sky.

About the Author

Al Maginnes was born in Massachusetts and raised in a number of states, mostly in the southeast. He has degrees in English and writing from East Carolina University and the University of Arkansas. A former recipient of a North Carolina Arts Council grant, he is the former music editor of *Connotations,* and his poems and reviews appear widely. He has taught at several colleges in North Carolina, including Louisburg College, where he is currently working.

I need to take a moment to thank many of those who touched and guided me on this journey, not only through this book, but on the often-rocky paths over the years. Some are not here to see this, and I miss their presence daily. And each of you deserves far more than a passing mention in the pages of a book: Betty Adcock, Randy Alley, Tom Aslin, Joseph Bathanti, Roy Bentley, Dixon Boyles, Christopher Buckley, Jim Clark, Suzanne Cleary, Floyd Collins, Grant Clauser, Malcolm and Cyndi Holcombe, Alan Kaufman, David Larson, Steve Larson, Sandy Longhorn, George Looney, RB Morris, Garnette Mullis, David Olney, Dale Ray Phillips, Dana Roeser, Ken and Kaite Roubidoux, Marty Silverthorne, June Sylvester Saraceno, Adam Tavel, Philip Terman, and David Weaver. My teachers Michael Heffernan, John Clellon Holmes, Peter Makuck, Heather Ross Miller, Jim Whitehead, and Miller Williams. All the editors who have taken chances on my work. All the ones I have forgotten or neglected here. And for my family who made all things possible